JOHANN SEBASTIAN BACH

DAVID WRIGHT ON HARPSICHORD AT
THE ARTS INSTITUTE AT BOURNEMOUTH
AND TEXT+WORK

EDITED BY VIOLET MCCLEAN
AND JOSEPHA SANNA

TEXT+WORK, THE GALLERY,
THE ARTS INSTITUTE AT BOURNEMOUTH

THE ARTS INSTITUTE AT BOURNEMOUTH AND TEXT+WORK

The Arts Institute at Bournemouth is one of only fifteen specialist higher education institutions in the UK devoted solely to the study of arts. The Institute has been providing specialist education for over a century and enjoys a strong reputation both nationally and internationally. www.aib.ac.uk

text+work is the concept which underpins the exhibition and creative events programme at the Arts Institute at Bournemouth. text+work promotes a forum for challenging dialogue between innovative contemporary arts, design and media practice and its theoretical context. www.textandwork.org.uk

The Arts Institute at Bournemouth is pleased to be able to host its first Music Event in association with text+work. This event is in aid of the Arts Institute at Bournemouth Charitable Foundation. The *Goldberg Variations* by Bach performed by David Wright, will mark the first occasion that the transferable concept text+work will support a Music Event. The *Goldberg Variations* are a set of 30 variations for harpsichord by Johann Sebastian Bach, named after Johann Gottlieb Goldberg who may have been the first performer.

THE ARTS INSTITUTE
AT BOURNEMOUTH
CHARITABLE FOUNDATION

The Foundation exists to support the improvement and enhancement of resources to benefit our students; the fund is used exclusively to support our student body and it is sourced through direct payments, gift aid, covenants and legacies.

We are immensely grateful to the generous donations from benefactors to date: alumni, past tutors, honorary fellows, parents and other individuals who have given their support. The Institute and its students thank those who have contributed; your support is much valued. The Institute wishes to acknowledge the generosity of the late Jean Hunnisett, Honorary Fellow of the Institute, for her endowment to Costume Design. We are also pleased to administer a memorial fund for Harriet Craigs, a student of Film, tragically killed in 2002; a prize by Anne Corkett, a former member of the academic staff; a Bursary in Cinematography on behalf of the Ossie Morris Foundation; and most recently, the Nigel Beale Award in Fashion Design.

To those who wish to contribute we welcome your support and ask that you contact our Finance Department for further details about donating to the Charitable Foundation.

e: finance@aib.ac.uk
t: 01202 363214

Contents

INTRODUCTION
PROFESSOR STUART BARTHOLOMEW

When the Gallery at the Arts Institute was enlarged and redesigned it was our hope that the new space would show work able to stimulate interest in creative practice within and beyond our academic community. The Gallery programme text+work has fulfilled this ambition and has now established itself as a significant regional centre for exhibition. The development of Institute House and the addition of a performance hall for recitals allows us to extend the text+work concept to both music and performance.

text+work was originated to make more enduring our exhibitions and performances. Ideas and commentary generated in words interact with those rooted in images or music. They form a critical discourse which can add measurably to the overall experience and record of events. The text by Terry Barfoot on JS Bach's *Goldberg Variations* is an example of this and complementary to the performance of this great work by David Wright on harpsichord.

The Arts Institute at Bournemouth is one of a small number of specialist providers of teaching, learning and scholarship in creative arts. It is pleased to extend its contribution to public provision through performances, and, in association with the Bournemouth Symphony Orchestra's contemporary music ensemble Kokora, will host a number of concerts in 2009.

Professor Stuart Bartholomew

JOHANN SEBASTIAN Bach (1685-1750)

By Terry Barfoot

Bach's supreme achievement was as a master of counterpoint, the simultaneous presentation of different musical lines. His ability to create complex webs of musical texture in strongly articulated fashion has remained unparalleled. His North German Protestant religion was the root of all his art, allied to a tireless industry in the pursuit of every kind of refinement of his skill and technique. Although some of the forms in which he wrote - the church cantata, for example - were outdated before he died, he poured into them all the resources of his genius so that they have outlived most other examples. As a composer of instrumental music Bach was ever willing to experiment, well beyond the possibilities offered by his own virtuosity as an organist and harpsichordist.

Bach's legacy of concertos, however, is relatively small in comparison with contemporary figures such as Telemann and Vivaldi; but this, of course, resulted from the nature of his career and the various posts which he held. From 1723 until his death in 1750 he was employed at Leipzig, where in addition to his duties at the Thomasschule and the two churches, the Thomaskirche and the Nikolaikirche, he directed the Collegium Musicum and its orchestral concerts. The repertoire in all these cases was contemporary, and in order to maximise the possibilities of his musical material he used 'parody', the musical tradition familiar from renaissance times of adapting existing compositions to serve new purposes. He did so to the extent, moreover, that this became a significant feature of his creative work. He was particularly influenced by Vivaldi, as well as by models from across Europe, and like other Baroque composers he was a great 'borrower', both from himself and from others. As a result, his works can exist in several versions, and sometimes can be partly based on existing material, not necessarily his own. But no matter, since his genius was such that his music remains truly indestructible, and can be performed satisfactorily in many different ways.

The cantatas are perhaps the most prolific part of Bach's output. Such are their qualities of invention and imagination, it is no exaggeration to consider them as music's greatest 'treasure trove'. They are particularly notable for their variety of structure, scoring and mood, since Bach was inspired by the religious imagery of the libretti to compose some of his finest music. The dramatic and emotional force of his music, as evidenced particularly in the Passions, was remarkable in its day and has spoken to succeeding generations with increasing power. For many listeners, therefore, Bach's music is supreme. Thus Richard Wagner's words retain their potency to this day: 'Bach is the most stupendous miracle in all music'.

BACH AND THE KEYBOARD

The most important influence in Bach's life was the Lutheran Church, which from the beginning was at the centre of his life. He soon became known as an excellent performer and improviser, and while he also played the violin on occasion at Weimar and held the position of Kappellmeister at the court at Cöthen, where he wrote much of his orchestral music, his chief work was in composing for the church and for the keyboard. His church cantatas, along with his organ music composed for church services, make up much of the largest part of his creative output. Chorale preludes and larger-scale organ works including preludes, toccatas or fantasias and fugues had clear associations with the church and its formalities.

As Cantor at Leipzig, working at the Thomaskirche and the Nikolaikirche from 1723, Bach's musical life was seldom free from problems and frustrations. With only limited resources available, he often made his frustrations known and became involved in heated debate with both the church and the town authorities. At the same time, during these years he composed what we now regard as his most significant music, although little of this was published during his lifetime. For example, this phase of his life brought forth the Mass in B Minor, the St Matthew Passion, the '48' Preludes and Fugues, and the four books of keyboard and organ music known as the *Clavier-Übung*, as well as *The Art of Fugue* and *The Musical Offering*.

With the dominating influence of the organ on the musicians of the German lands, it is hardly surprising that harpsichord design and construction were strongly influenced by the organ. The single-manual Italian harpsichords of the period had a percussive tone that was ideally suited to continuo playing in ensemble music, while the more decorative French two-manual instruments sounded the rich sonorities associated with the music of François Couperin. The main German harpsichord-makers, such as Hieronymus Haas, built instruments that offered an altogether wider range of sonorities. At the same time they developed the pedal harpsichord, and there is evidence that Bach owned at least one of these instruments. He played the clavichord also, a domestic keyboard instrument that was popular in Germany, and he preferred to use it during the course of his creative work. In contrast to the full-toned organ, this instrument was able to produce restrained and subtle changes of dynamic and of pitch.

Bach's magnificent collection of organ music divides into four categories:

01
Chorale Preludes
These short compositions are based on existing chorale melodies (the hymn tunes of the Lutheran church), decorating and embellishing the original melody. They vary considerably in tempo and character.

02
Preludes and fugues, toccatas and fugues, fantasias and fugues
These are compositions on the larger scale, especially if the first movement is followed by a companion fugue. In other cases, the preludes, toccatas, fantasias, or fugues exist as separate movements.

03
Trios and duets
The trios have three lines of music performed using the two manuals and the pedals, while the duets employ only the two manuals.

04
Transcriptions of instrumental concertos by other composers
These include for example several of the concertos from L'Estro Armonico, Opus 3, by Vivaldi.

Bach grouped 21 of his chorale preludes and the 4 Duetts, framing them with the celebrated St Anne Prelude and Fugue in E flat major, and published the collection as *Clavier-Übung* Part III (Keyboard Practice Part III). Other collections of chorale preludes were the *Orgel-Büchlein* and *the Schübler Chorales*.

Bach's most significant collections of music for solo keyboard, either harpsichord or clavichord, are:

- **The 15 Two-part Inventions and 15 Three-part Inventions (sometimes described as *Sinfonias*)**

- **The 6 French Suites, 6 *English Suites*, and 6 *Partitas* (these form the *Clavier-Übung* Part I)**

- **The *French Overture* in B minor and the *Italian Concerto* (these form the *Clavier-Übung* Part II)**

- **The two sets of 24 Preludes and Fugues, known as *The Well-tempered Clavier* (the '48' Preludes and Fugues)**

- **The *Goldberg Variations* (*Clavier-Übung Part IV*)**

In addition, Bach also composed numerous other pieces, including several toccatas, the *Anna Magdalena Notebook*, and transcriptions of concertos for harpsichord by Vivaldi, Marcello and even the Duke of Saxe-Weimar. Only in a few cases, such as the designation of the harpsichord for the *Italian Concerto* and the *Goldberg Variations*, does Bach specify the details of the instrument to be employed. Otherwise he believed the music to be equally appropriate for either the harpsichord or the clavichord, while some compositions might alternatively be played on the organ.

GOLDBERG VARIATIONS, BWV 988

rom 1723 Bach worked at Leipzig, in the employment of the Town Council. However, throughout the 1730s and 1740s his links with Dresden, though informal and occasional, were also of significance. One example of this was the sponsorship he received from Count Hermann von Keyserlingk, to whom he presented the first bound edition of the *Goldberg Variations* during a visit to Dresden in October 1741.

The Count's resident harpsichordist was Gottlieb Goldberg (1727-1756), who was a particularly gifted player, and an occasional pupil of both Bach and his son Wilhelm Friedemann. There is evidence to suggest that in due course Goldberg developed the habit of playing the *Variations* to help his master endure the night hours during his frequent bouts of insomnia.

Be that as it may, no formal dedication was recorded on the printed score. It seems likely therefore that Bach composed the *Variations* for himself and only subsequently offered them to the Count and Goldberg, who was then aged just fourteen, because it seemed expedient to do so. The music also forms the final part of Bach's great collection the *Clavier-Übung* (Keyboard Practice), a collection of exercises in keyboard playing. The contents included the most important types of keyboard music contained in exemplary and imaginative compositions.

As a carefully contrived sequence of short pieces, the *Goldberg Variations* closes one chapter of Bach's creative life, while at the same time opening another. In this sense the music's importance can be recognised for the simple reason that it forms the first of the monothematic, contrapuntal and purely instrumental works which dominated the final decade of his life. Bach's manuscript was discovered only as recently as 1975, and it was found to contain an appendix 'with 14 canons on the first 8 ground notes of the aria'. This new intellectual concept recurs also in several later works, including for example the *Musical Offering*.

The *Goldberg Variations* are notable for their perfection of form. The general plan reflects Bach's intended balance of 'inventio' and 'ratio'. Moreover the variety of musical forms, types of rhythmic movement, expressive moods and technical refinements divide the work into two large sections, each of 15 variations. As if to confirm this, the second half begins with an overture, and like the first half the sequence of movements proceeds to a richly contrapuntal climax. Each third section is a canon, with the intervals of the imitations widening steadily to the extreme of a ninth. At the close there stands a quodlibet, making a lively final phase in which the principal theme combines with aspects of folk song. After these many and varied approaches, the return of the aria - that is, the original theme - is as direct as it is sublime.

ARIA (THEME)

Variation 01
Three-four time. Two voice invention, *courante* style. Hand-crossing. Single manual.

Variation 02
Two-four time. Imitative as trio sonata (eg two violins and bass). Two manual keyboard.

Variation 03
Twelve-eight time. Two voice canon at the unison with an independent bass line. The upper voice commences one phrase (bar) after the lower voice. Single manual keyboard.

Variation 04
Three-eight time. *Passepied*. The image is 'leaping dance music'. Four voices. Single manual.

Variation 05
Three-four time. Two voice invention which requires crossing of the hands. Single or two manual keyboard.

Variation 06
Three-eight time. Two voice canon at the second interval with an independent bass line. The upper voice enters one phrase (bar) after the lower one. Single manual keyboard.

Variation 07
Six-eight time. Two voice *Gigue*. Single or two manual keyboard.

Variation 08
Three-four time. Free style variation. Two voice invention, which requires crossing of the hands. Two manual keyboard.

Variation 09
Common time. Two voice canon at the three with an independent bass line. The upper voice commences a phrase (bar) after the lower voice. Single manual keyboard.

Variation 10

Two-two time. Free style variation. Four voice fugheta. Single manual keyboard.

Variation 11

Twelve-sixteen time. Two voice *gigue* style which requires crossing of the hands. Two manual keyboard.

Variation 12

Three-Four time. Two voice *inversus* canon at the fourth. Right and left sides of the lower voice is reversed on the upper voice and start one phrase (bar) after. Single manual keyboard.

Variation 13

Three-four time. Free melodic variation *sarabande* style. Two manual keyboard.

Variation 14

Three-four time. Virtuoso hand-crossing. Two voice parts. Two manual keyboard.

Variation 15

Two-four time. G minor andante. Canon inversus at the fifth interval. Single manual keyboard.

Variation 16

Half way point marked with a Grand French Overture style opening, followed by *stretto fugue* in three-eight time. Single manual keyboard.

Variation 17

Three-four time. Two voice hand-crossing similar to Variation 14. Two manual keyboard.

Variation 18

Two-two time. Two voice canon at the sixth interval. Trio sonata style. The upper voice commences a half a bar after the lower voice. Single manual keyboard.

Variation 19

Three-eight time. Free style variation, *minuet* style. Single manual keyboard.

Variation 20

Three-four time. Duet requiring crossing of hands with great skill. Two manual keyboard.

Variation 21

Common time. G minor. Two voice canon at the seventh interval with free chromatic scale bass. The upper voice commences a half a bar after the lower voice. Single manual keyboard.

Variation 22

Two-two time. Four voice *gavotte*-like rhythm. Fugato style. Single manual keyboard.

Variation 23

Three-four time. Two and three voice, requiring difficult crossing of hands. Two manual keyboard.

Variation 24

Nine-eight time. Two voice canon at the octave. Pastoral *siciliano* style. The upper voice commences two bars after the lower voice. Single manual keyboard.

Variation 25

Nine-eight time. Free style G minor variation. Adagio. Decorated Aria develops over the two voice chromatic scale bass. Two manual keyboard.

Variation 26

Eighteen-sixteen time. Three voice parts. *Sarabande* with hand-crossing. Two manual keyboard.

Variation 27

Six-eight time. Two voiced canon at the ninth. *Gigue-like*. Single manual keyboard.

Variation 28

Three Four time. Difficult hand-crossing with trills. Two manual keyboard.

Variation 29

Three-four time. Rapid hand alternating chords, Single manual keyboard.

Variation 30

Common time. Four voice parts. Three voice *quodlibet* with a free style bass. Here is combined the theme of the work, bass line and two folktunes: *'Kraut und Ruben haben mich vertieben'* and *'Ich bin so lang nicht bei dir g'west'*. Single manual keyboard.

Aria da capo

CONTEMPORARY ART AND THE *Goldberg* VARIATIONS

By Josepha Sanna

In 2007, the artist Cory Arcangel made the film *A Couple Thousand Short Films About Glenn Gould* in which he rescored *J.S Bach's Goldberg Variations* by splicing together almost 2,000 clips of amateur musicians' performances from video-sharing websites such as YouTube. This hypnotising split-screen video work sees the unintentional collaboration of anonymous guitarists, tuba players, keyboard players, and others, to recreate this classical piece of music—a democratic art piece, truly, and one that re-connects and connects us to Bach, giving the composer and *Goldberg Variations* the opportunity for a revival and renewed historical relevance. In the same year, David Wright released his recording J.S Bach, *Goldberg Variations* on ZUM Records, to great acclaim. This recording was praised for, amongst many other things, giving the listener the impression that he/she is hearing something quite new—a quality especially important when approaching a very familiar work already many times recorded. These two artists - one a musician and one a video artist, both working in different disciplines - manage to communicate to their respective audiences a new and refreshing way of experiencing the classical composer's *Goldberg Variations*, each re-educating our eyes and ears.

The meeting of music and art is far from uncommon: in 2004, Dan Fox[1] spoke of the art world's continuing and enduring fascination with music, citing the composer Ligeti and his association with the Fluxus movement in the 1960s, and John Cage's friendship with the artists Robert Rauschenberg and Jasper Johns. Indeed, *Goldberg Variations* by David Wright at the Arts Institute at Bournemouth coincides with Sam Taylor Wood's screening of *Sigh*[2] at the White Cube Mason's Yard, and, in a more recent essay, critic David Briers[3] draws links between contemporary music and visual art, commenting on the similarities between the contemporary music festivals' and the galleries' completely silent and reverential audiences; he discusses the centres opening up to accommodate music and the visual arts[4] , and contemporary music as 'sheer spectacle', sufficient in itself.

Coming to classical music from the perspective of one trained and working in the visual arts can prove to be slightly problematic and somewhat of a challenge: now that one has learnt to look one must learn to listen. By hosting and attending events such as *Goldberg Variations* performed by David Wright, we can not only give classical music the opportunity for renewed historical relevance and enjoy this discipline in its own right, we can also grasp the historical relevance behind contemporary visual art pieces such as Cory Arcangel's *A Couple Thousand Short Films About Glenn Gould.*

1 Fox, D. 'Could Contemporary Art's Engagement with Music be More Adventurous?' *Frieze Magazine*, Issue 84, June-August 2004

2 Sam Taylor Wood's *Sigh* sees 100 members of the BBC's Concert Orchestra mime the playing of instruments to a specially commissioned score by Academy Award-winning composer Anne Dudley. The exhibition runs 24 October - 5 November 2008 at White Cube Mason's Yard.

3 Briers, D. 'Art & Music', *Art Monthly*, No313, February 2008

4 Examples include the recently opened Kings Place, London, and, closer to home, Lighthouse, Poole.

David graduated with distinction from the Royal College of Music in 2003 where for two consecutive years he won the Richard the Third and Century Fund Prizes. In the same year he also won first prize in the prestigious Broadwood Harpsichord Competition - an international event held biannually at London's Fenton House, home of the Historic Benton Fletcher collection of early keyboard instruments, where he subsequently became artist in residence.

Born in Bethnal Green in the East End of London, David Wright received no musical training as a child and taught himself to play 'by ear'. It wasn't until he was sixteen that he had his first piano lesson and learned to read music, later going on to study harpsichord, organ, and viola da gamba as an undergraduate

at Trinity College of Music, where he won the Ella Kidney prize for early music. David works regularly with some of the world's leading ensembles and musicians. He has directed concerts from the harpsichord including the first modern performance of Thomas Arne's ballard opera 'The Blind Beggar of Bethnal Green'.

David is engaged regularly amongst the artists at Dartington International Summer School and as repetitieur with the English Touring Opera and The English Bach Festival, with whom he has been assistant musical director for several operas. David's radio and television broadcasts include performances as a finalist in the York Early Music Competition and soloist at the Handel House Museum London (both for BBC Radio3) and more recently a recital as part of the Belfast Music Festival, broadcast on BBC Northern Ireland. As a continuo player and soloist David performs regularly with the London Concertante, who tour extensively worldwide.

David's new recording of Bach's *Goldberg Variations* was released on the 1st of May 2007 with a complete performance of them at St Martin-in-the-Fields, which attracted the attention of the ITV news, who featured the concert in the headlines that evening.

Recent engagements include the world premiere with Emma Kirkby of a new work by Stephen Mcneff, the first modern performance of a Harpsichord concerto by J.H.Roman (1694-1757) with his new baroque orchestra 'The Harmonious Society of Tickle-Fiddle Gentlemen' (July 2008), Bach's D minor concerto with the London Concertant (September 2008), and harpsichord concertos by Arne and Stanley with Peter Holman (August 2008). David also has a number of performances of the *Goldberg Variations* coming up, details of which can be found on his website: **www.wrightnotes.com**

David has a keen interest in instrument building and restoration, and has recently completed a copy of a 17th century English harpsichord which he uses regularly for concerts.